What a M

by Kaye Umansky

THE CAST

BEN **SAM**

MOUSE **JOJO**

Scene 1

The secret room.

Enter Sam, Ben, Jojo and Mouse.

BEN What a mess!

SAM How did it get like this?

MOUSE Look at the twigs!

JOJO And who ate all the biscuits?

BEN Not me!

MOUSE Not me!

SAM Not me!

BEN We must clean it up.

MOUSE We can get some things from our house.

All exit.

Scene 2

The twins' kitchen.

Enter Ben, Sam, Jojo and Mouse.

JOJO   We need a broom.

MOUSE   And a dustpan.

SAM   I'll take a bucket.

BEN   Where are the dusters, Jojo?

JOJO   Sssh! My mum will hear.

BEN   Will she mind if we take these things?

MOUSE   No, but she will ask why we need them.

SAM   We must keep our room a secret. Come on.

All tiptoe out.

Scene 3

The secret room.

Enter Ben, Sam, Mouse and Jojo.

BEN We must shake out the carpet.

SAM I'll help you, Ben.

JOJO I'll pick some new flowers.

Exit Jojo, with the dead flowers.

MOUSE I'll sweep the floor.

SAM Look at the dust!

BEN Atchoo!

MOUSE There goes a spider!

SAM Do you think he ate the biscuits?

BEN Spiders don't eat biscuits, silly.

Enter Jojo, with some flowers.

JOJO Here are the flowers.

BEN Can you pass the duster, Sam?

SAM The carpet looks much better now.

MOUSE This is more fun than cleaning our bedroom.

They finish cleaning.

BEN There. All done.

JOJO It looks good again.

SAM That was hard work.

BEN We must take the things back.

MOUSE Then we can play.

All exit.

Scene 4

The next day in the secret room. There are more twigs on the floor.

Enter Ben, Sam, Mouse and Jojo.

BEN Oh, no! How did this mess get here?

SAM Look at the floor! More twigs!

MOUSE I spent ages sweeping it, too.

JOJO Who has been here?

BEN Do you think Grumpyboots has found our room?

JOJO Oh no!

MOUSE Our room is not a secret any more.

BEN But it's not like Grumpyboots to make a mess.

SAM Ben is right. And Grumpyboots is too old to crawl under the bushes.

JOJO Who did it, then?

MOUSE Sssh!

BEN What?

MOUSE I hear something.

They all listen.

JOJO I can't hear a thing.

BEN What did you hear, Mouse?

MOUSE A sort of tweet. It came from up there.

He points up.

BEN   Yes! I can hear it too.

SAM   What is up there?

JOJO   It is too dark to see.

MOUSE   Help! What is it?

BEN   I'll stand on the table and look.

JOJO   Mind the flowers!

Jojo takes the jug off. Ben stands on the table.

SAM   What is it? Can you see?

BEN   Wait! Hold my legs! Pass up the torch, Mouse.

MOUSE   Here.

He passes up the torch.

Ben shines the torch into a dark corner.

BEN Aha! I see a nest! It's full of baby birds!

SAM Oh, how lovely.

The mother bird enters through the window.

MOUSE Mind out! Here comes mum!

The bird flaps about. Ben jumps down.

BEN So that is who has been dropping twigs all over the floor.

MOUSE And eating all our biscuits!

The End